America's Animal Soldiers

Dolphins in the NAVY

by Meish Goldish

Consultant: Sam Ridgway DVM, PhD, DACZM
President, National Marine Mammal Foundation
San Diego, California

BEARPORT PUBLISHING

New York, New York

Credits

Cover and Title Page, © Kristian Sekulic/iStockphoto and U.S. Navy; 4, © U.S. Navy/Photographer's Mate 1st Class Brien Aho; 5, © U.S. Navy/Photographer's Mate 1st Class Brien Aho; 6, © U.S. Navy/Mass Communication Specialist 2nd Class Jennifer A. Villalovos; 8, © AP Photo/Greg Gibson; 9, Courtesy of The National Marine Mammal Foundation; 10, © U.S. Navy/Mass Communication Specialist Hodges Pone III; 11, © Justin Sullivan/Getty Images; 12, © AP Photo/The Virginian-Pilot/Steve Earley; 13, © AP Photo/The Virginian-Pilot/Steve Earley; 14, © Courtesy of The National Marine Mammal Foundation; 15, © U.S. Navy/Photographer's Mate 1st Class Brien Aho; 16, © Augusto Stanzani/Ardea; 17, © K Guymer/Newspix/Rex USA/BEImages; 18T, © U.S. Navy/Photographer's Mate 2nd Class Bob Houlihan; 18B, © Courtesy of The National Marine Mammal Foundation; 20, © U.S. Navy/Photographer's Mate 2nd Class Michael Sandberg; 21, © AP Photo/US Navy/Jason Trevett; 22, © Kristian Sekulic/iStockphoto; 23, © Markabond/Shutterstock.

Publisher: Kenn Goin
Editorial Director: Adam Siegel
Creative Director: Spencer Brinker
Design: Debrah Kaiser
Photo Researcher: Picture Perfect Professionals, LLC

Library of Congress Cataloging-in-Publication Data

Goldish, Meish.
  Dolphins in the Navy / by Meish Goldish ; consultant, Sam Ridgway.
      p. cm. — (America's animal soldiers)
  Audience: Ages 7–12.
  Includes bibliographical references and index.
  ISBN-13: 978-1-61772-451-0 (library binding)
  ISBN-10: 1-61772-451-3 (library binding)
  1. Bottlenose dolphin—War use—Juvenile literature. 2. United States. Navy—History—21st century—Juvenile literature. I. Ridgway, Sam H. II. Title.
  UH100.5.B68G65 2012
  359—dc23

                                            2011034461

For more information, write to Bearport Publishing Company, Inc., 45 West 21st Street, Suite 3B, New York, New York 10010. Printed in the United States of America in North Mankato, Minnesota.

10 9 8 7 6 5 4 3 2 1

CONTENTS

K-Dog on Duty

K-Dog swam quickly through the waters of the **Persian Gulf**. He had an important job to do. In 2003 the United States was at war with Iraq. American, British, and Australian ships carrying thousands of tons of food and other supplies needed to reach an Iraqi **port**. The enemy, however, had hidden **sea mines** in the water. K-Dog had to find the bombs so that they didn't explode and destroy the ships when they arrived.

K-Dog leaps out of the Persian Gulf. He wears equipment on his flipper that lets Navy workers know his underwater location.

A sea mine is a kind of bomb placed in the water by swimmers who are trying to blow up enemy ships and submarines.

Although K-Dog's name might make people think he is a dog, the **expert** swimmer is actually a bottlenose dolphin. He was trained by the U.S. Navy to locate underwater dangers. K-Dog and several other dolphins helped find more than 100 mines around the Iraqi port. Human divers then **disabled** each one. Within a week, the supply ships were able to **dock** safely thanks to the dolphins' skillful work.

K-Dog rides back to base after a day of hard work.

Now Hear This

K-Dog is one of about 75 bottlenose dolphins that work for the U.S. Navy. They are trained, along with California sea lions, to protect ocean and **coastal** waters. The animals are part of the U.S. Navy **Marine Mammal** Program, based in San Diego, California. Why does the Navy use dolphins to locate sea mines? One reason is because of the animal's special ability to find things in the water—which is called **echolocation.**

In the wild, dolphins use echolocation to find fish and other **prey**. The Navy, however, has taught the animals to find sea mines using this special skill.

Katrina is one of the dolphins in the Marine Mammal Program that is trained to find sea mines.

When a dolphin uses echolocation, it first makes clicking sounds. These sounds bounce off objects and return to the dolphin. The bouncing sounds are called **echoes**. Dolphins can tell the size, shape, and location of an object by listening to them. If an echo bounces back quickly, a dolphin knows an object is near. If the echo takes longer to hear, the object is farther away.

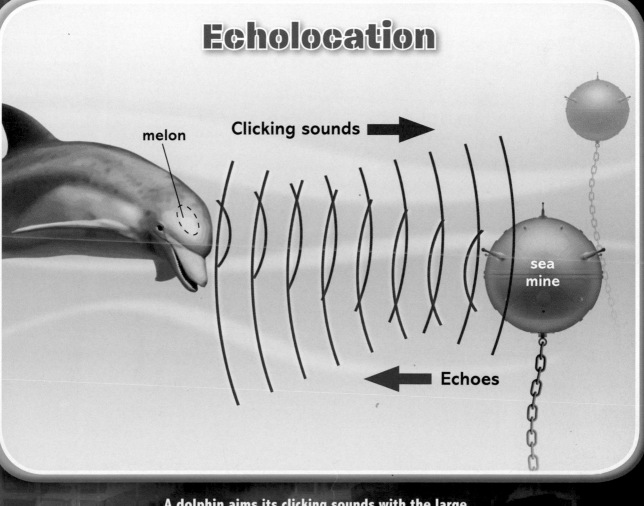

Echolocation

melon

Clicking sounds ➡️

sea mine

⬅️ **Echoes**

A dolphin aims its clicking sounds with the large, rounded part of its head, called the melon.

Finding Mines

A Navy dolphin is trained to use echolocation to find sea mines of all shapes and sizes. The mines could be buried under sand, sitting on the ocean floor, or **suspended** in the water. Using echolocation, a dolphin can locate a sea mine in a matter of minutes. Human divers might take weeks to find the same mine.

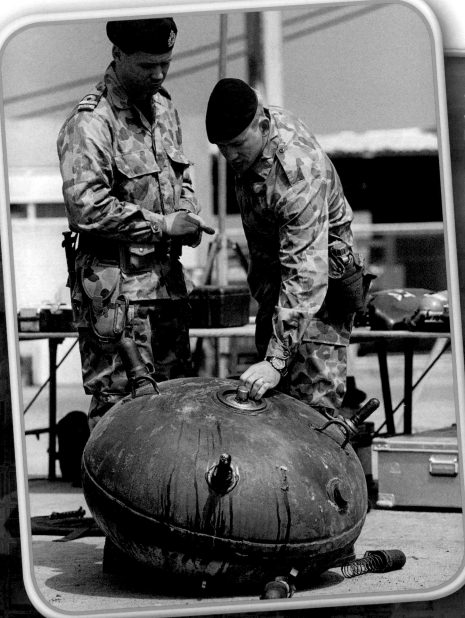

This sea mine was found in the Persian Gulf.

After a dolphin finds an object that could be a mine, the animal swims to the boat where its **handler** is waiting. The dolphin touches a tennis ball or plastic disk at the front of the boat. This means, "I've found something." The handler then gives the dolphin a floating **marker** to place near the object so that people can find it. Next, a Navy diver enters the water to inspect what the dolphin has found. If it is a mine, the diver will disable it.

Using echolocation, a bottlenose dolphin can find a sea mine as far away as 150 yards (137 m). That's the length of one and a half football fields.

This bottlenose dolphin is placing a yellow marker next to a mine it has found.

Hide-and-Seek

A Navy dolphin is trained to find more than just mines. It also searches for people—possible **terrorists**—who are swimming in the water. After finding a swimmer, the dolphin returns to its boat. The handler then places a **strobe light** or noisemaker on the animal's nose. Next, the dolphin returns to the water to finish its job.

Bottlenose dolphins protect Naval Base Kitsap near Seattle, Washington. They search for terrorists who may try to destroy the Navy's ships and submarines.

The dolphin quietly sneaks up on the swimmer. It bumps into the person from behind in order to knock loose the handler's **device** from its nose and attach it to the swimmer's air tank. Navy divers then use the device to locate and capture the person in the water.

Bottlenose dolphins are trained only to mark a swimmer's location. They never attack or try to capture the person in the water.

Dolphins aren't the only ones that need to learn how to catch terrorists. As part of their training, these officers practice pulling in swimmers who are pretending to be enemy divers.

Handle with Care

Handlers treat their dolphins with great care. For example, Navy officer Andres Palacio works with a bottlenose dolphin named Puts. Palacio knows that dolphins love to be touched. He often rubs Puts's belly to keep her happy. When he is training the clever animal, he rewards the dolphin with small fish for correct behavior.

Andres Palacio treats Puts to a belly rub.

A Navy handler never punishes a bottlenose dolphin if it performs poorly in the water. Instead, the handler ignores the wrong action and works to correct it through more practice.

Palacio knows that dolphins, like human beings, have different moods. "You feel their **body language** and you know when they're **motivated**, when they're happy, when they're sad," he said. Puts can also sense her handler's mood. Once, Palacio cut his hand and was in pain. Puts swam up and rested her nose in Palacio's lap to comfort him.

Palacio gives Puts fish when she performs well.

Staying Healthy

Handlers aren't the only people who take good care of the Navy's bottlenose dolphins. **Veterinarians** check the animals every day to make sure each dolphin is healthy and strong. The doctors begin by inspecting the mammal's teeth, which get brushed regularly.

A bottlenose dolphin getting its tongue and teeth brushed

The dolphins are taught to relax so vets can perform other exams as well. When a dolphin seems ill, a vet takes the animal's temperature and draws its blood for tests that determine if the dolphin is sick. A vet also places a **stethoscope** under the animal's flipper to check its heart rate and listen to its breathing. Whenever the dolphins travel by boat or plane, medical equipment is brought along. Vets use it to check the animals for illness.

A Navy veterinarian is on call 24 hours a day, 7 days a week, for the animals in the Navy Marine Mammal Program.

Hefi, a Navy dolphin, getting a medical examination

Keeping Dolphins Safe

Although the Navy takes great effort to care for its dolphins, not everyone is pleased with the Marine Mammal Program. Some animal lovers argue it is unfair to use dolphins for dangerous work. The Navy, however, says the animals are never placed in risky situations.

Sea mines are made to explode when ships pass by. A dolphin weighs too little to cause a mine to explode.

For example, the Navy makes sure that the dolphins are far away and safe by the time mines are disabled or swimmers are captured. According to Navy officials, dolphins that work for the Marine Mammal Program are in less danger from their work than those that live in the wild—which may be killed and eaten by sharks or fed unsafe food by people.

This wild bottlenose dolphin was attacked by a shark.

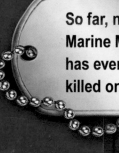

So far, no animal in the Marine Mammal Program has ever been injured or killed on the job.

Past and Present

When the Navy Marine Mammal Program began in 1960, it trained only bottlenose dolphins. However, it soon began to work with California sea lions as well. Both of these sea mammals are very smart. As a result, they learn new skills very easily. It wasn't long before dolphins successfully served in the Vietnam War (1957–1975) in the 1970s and then in the Persian Gulf in the 1980s.

This sea lion is trained to find enemy divers.

A baby dolphin swimming near its mother

The Navy Marine Mammal Program starts training some dolphins when they are just a few months old. They don't become mine hunters, however, until they are several years old.

During the 2000s, both sea lions and dolphins served in the Persian Gulf. Once there, they searched for sea mines and enemy divers. How did the animals get to such a faraway place? They were flown from San Diego on U.S. Air Force transport planes. In fact, the Navy's dolphins and sea lions can be **deployed** anywhere in the world within 72 hours. They are transported by ships, helicopters, or airplanes.

Arctic Ocean

ASIA

NORTH AMERICA

Atlantic Ocean

EUROPE

Pacific Ocean

AFRICA

Persian Gulf

Pacific Ocean

SOUTH AMERICA

Indian Ocean

AUSTRALIA

N
W E
S

Where Navy marine mammals have been deployed

Southern Ocean

ANTARCTICA

The purple parts of this map show the places where animals from the Navy Marine Mammal Program have served.

The Future for Navy Dolphins

Will robots ever be able to match the underwater skills of bottlenose dolphins? Some **experts** doubt it. However, in 2010 the Navy announced that a new robot had been developed. It's called an **unmanned underwater vehicle**, or UUV. Navy officials think it may be able to replace bottlenose dolphins in the future.

This robotic device is used to find underwater mines.

A UUV can work for 70 hours at a time and in waters that are almost 2,000 feet (610 m) deep.

A UUV looks like a small submarine. Inside, it holds equipment that is able to find sea mines. The UUV sends information it gathers from the ocean floor to humans on the water's surface. Only time will tell if this new robot will succeed. In the meantime, bottlenose dolphins will remain on duty. They will continue to play an important role in helping to keep America safe.

More About
Bottlenose Dolphins

Some bottlenose dolphins work for the U.S. Navy.
However, most of these mammals live in the wild.
Here is some more information about them.

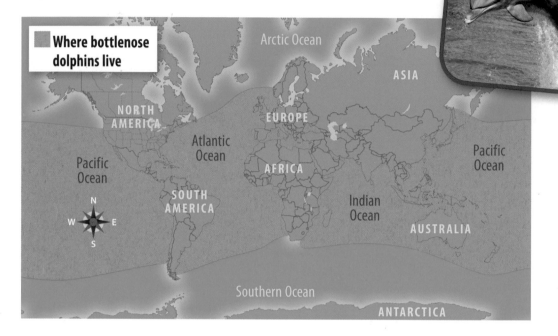

Where bottlenose dolphins live

Weight	330–775 pounds (150–352 kg)
Length	6–13 feet (2–4 m)
Life Span	25–30 years, though some may live to 50 years or even more
Average Speed	3–6 miles per hour (5–10 kph), but they can reach speeds of 21 miles per hour (34 kph)
Food	mainly fish and squid
Habitat	all major oceans and seas of the world except the Arctic and Southern Oceans
Predators	large shark species, such as tiger sharks, great white sharks, dusky sharks, and bull sharks

Glossary

body language (BOD-ee LANG-wij) a message suggested by the way a person or animal sits, stands, or moves his or her body

coastal (KOHST-uhl) having to do with land that runs along an ocean

deployed (di-PLOYD) sent to an area for a specific purpose

device (di-VYESS) a piece of equipment that does a particular job

disabled (diss-AY-buhld) took away the ability to do something

dock (DOK) to bring a ship to a landing area, such as a pier

echoes (EK-ohz) sounds that bounce off an object and return to the place where they came from

echolocation (*ek*-oh-loh-KAY-shuhn) a method for finding an object's position by sending out sounds that bounce back to the sender

expert (EK-spurt) highly skilled

experts (EK-spurts) people who know a lot about a subject

handler (HAND-lur) a person who works with animals

marine mammal (muh-REEN MAM-uhl) a warm-blooded animal that lives in the ocean, has whiskers, hair, or fur on its skin at some point in its life, and drinks its mother's milk as a baby

marker (MARK-ur) an object used to show the position of something

motivated (MOH-tuh-*vay*-tid) encouraged or excited to do something

Persian Gulf (PUR-zhuhn GUHLF) a body of water in southwestern Asia that is surrounded by several countries, including Saudi Arabia, Iran, and Iraq

port (PORT) a place where boats and ships can dock safely

prey (PRAY) animals that are hunted and eaten by other animals

sea mines (SEE MYENZ) bombs placed underwater

stethoscope (STETH-uh-*skohp*) an instrument that doctors use to listen to a patient's heart and lungs

strobe light (STROHB LITE) a bright light that flashes on and off very quickly

suspended (suh-SPEN-did) held in place; hanging in the water or air

terrorists (TER-ur-ists) people who use violence and threats to frighten others into obeying them

unmanned underwater vehicle (UN-*mand uhn*-dur-WAW-tur VEE-uh-kuhl) a submarine-like device that is used to locate sea mines, swimmers, submarines, and other objects in the water

veterinarians (*vet*-ur-uh-NAIR-ee-uhnz) doctors who treat sick or injured animals

Index

Bibliography

Dudzinski, Kathleen M., and Toni Frohoff. *Dolphin Mysteries: Unlocking the Secrets of Communication.* New Haven, CT: Yale University Press (2010).

Kistler, John M. *Animals in the Military: From Hannibal's Elephants to the Dolphins of the U.S. Navy.* Santa Barbara, CA: ABC-CLIO (2011).

Le Chêne, Evelyn. *Silent Heroes: The Bravery and Devotion of Animals in War.* London: Souvenir Press (2009).

Reynolds, John E., Randall S. Wells, and Samantha D. Eide. *The Bottlenose Dolphin: Biology and Conservation.* Gainesville, FL: University Press of Florida (2000).

U.S. Navy Marine Mammal Program (www.public.navy.mil/spawar/Pacific/71500/Pages/default.aspx)

Read More

Goldish, Meish. *Sea Lions in the Navy (America's Animal Soldiers).* New York: Bearport (2012).

Ingram, Scott. *Dolphins (Smart Animals!).* New York: Bearport (2006).

Murray, Julie. *Military Animals (Going to Work).* Edina, MN: ABDO (2009).

Presnall, Judith Janda. *Navy Dolphins (Animals with Jobs).* San Diego, CA: KidHaven Press (2002).

Learn More Online

To learn more about bottlenose dolphins in the U.S. Navy, visit
www.bearportpublishing.com/AmericasAnimalSoldiers

About the Author

Meish Goldish has written more than 200 books for children. He lives in Brooklyn, New York.